THE GARDEN OF SLENDER TRUST

CHRISTIANIA WHITEHEAD

The GARDEN
of SLENDER
TRUST

BLOODAXE BOOKS

ISBN: 1 85224 482 8

First published 1999 by
Bloodaxe Books Ltd,
P.O. Box 1SN,
Newcastle upon Tyne NE99 1SN.

Bloodaxe Books Ltd acknowledges
the financial assistance of Northern Arts.

Cover printing by J. Thomson Colour Printers Ltd, Glasgow.

Printed in Great Britain by
Cromwell Press Ltd, Trowbridge, Wiltshire.

And whan I had a while goon,
I saugh a gardyn right anoon,
Ful long and brood, and everydell
Enclosed was, and walled well
With highe walles enbatailled,
Portraied without and wel entailled
With many riche portraitures.
And bothe the ymages and the peyntures
Gan I biholde bysyly.

GEOFFREY CHAUCER (trans.),
The Romaunt of the Rose

Acknowledgements

Acknowledgements are due to the editors of the following publications in which some of these poems first appeared: *Bossy Parrot* (Bloodaxe Books, 1987), *New Women Poets* (Bloodaxe Books, 1990) and *Oxford Poetry*.

Some of these poems were included in a collection for which Christiania Whitehead received an Eric Gregory Award from the Society of Authors in 1998.

Contents

Horrible Gardens

How horrible the gardens are.
All the plants signifying the virtues
have got muddled, and are passing on
leaves to each other, and tearing
each other up, and there is no longer
the faintest remainder
of colour sense.

My sterling boy, who used to be
always out there – with so much
morality under his fingernails
that he seemed mildly crucified –
has turned over.
         His head is between
his legs, he has developed a hundred fingers
for telling lies upon. His belly
has depressed into deception
as against concern.

When he picks plants, he is not
picking the virtue he thinks he is
for they have changed roots overnight.
Things which were golden and plain
have transfused into charlatans.
A sense of trust became so black and hot
inside that her petals fell off.

Oh my son, my brother, who sanctioned
plant clothes and brought round flowers
until I started to believe, how can your severe
priestly understanding have faltered into levity?
How can the eucharists we used to find
in all our food have shrunk so fast?
In the sky I see now not one hand but two:
old mother Fortune, repealing virtues,
breaking bread to cinders and instructing
all the bright crusts to forsake their wedded past.

The House of St Gregory and St Macrina

Russian madames, darkly grand
and flanked with carrier bags, donated
drawers and tables from their steppe
estates to dress this home.

The black wood stretched workmen,
shrunk the colourfulness of student
penny spines, made their readers
sober, watchful internationals

expecting Balkan valkyrie to goad
their sleep. I've lavished love here
for this salted holiness. The spiders,
climbing on metal which nips in

the icons, acknowledge the sanctity
of their aerial roost. The severe
carpets proceed many times
to the seasoned face of a patriarch.

In the library, behind grills,
a crackling deposit of lore gets
leafed and left for mould by
ardent men. The garden, thrown

behind this height, is dried, full
of flat slates timing or interpreting
the sun. The plants crack
with unEnglish pride. Heaven

is involved with the lawn
which is dusty white. The pears
standing from the fruit trees
revile their own weight. A plump

orthodox scene is at home
in all this; its church quietly
weaves languages and enacts
journeys. Its guardians

trim their beards over the soil.
Its pictures are strong and compelling
enough to receive kisses; they eject
colour into the octagonal tenement

of god. The saintly two, touching
unseen cheeks with joy, are probably
gone between house and church.
Their shy fingers swell the stony fruit

in the late summer. And their probing
moves the residents' humour to exhibit
love. Gregory stands on the left.
His mitre left elsewhere, splendidly

a brother. Macrina rocks something
in her arms, sisterliness
in evidence, her habit falling
in long tiers about her stem.

The House of St Gregory and St Macrina: An Orthodox community for
students. An Orthodox church stands in its garden.
St Gregory and St Macrina: sister and brother, bishop and nun, early saints
within the Orthodox calendar.

The Unicorn is a Symbol of Virginity

Dun brown tomorrow. The unicorn
looks surprised. It had faintly expected
always to stay white.

'Does that mean my horn will
creep back into my head?' whimpers
the miscreant, and it paws the ground

a little, as if in protest.
Tush, rocking horse! You have nothing
but milk teeth to talk with,

you are only the little creature
the woman chuckles with,
when she is feeling holy.

Perched there amongst
the shamrocks and thorn roses –
you were never meant to last,

but came down through the ages
on a prayer cushion or in locket form,
eluding the bonny cavalry

by dint of a streak up a tree.
Mother of Jesus, what did you start?
Of course the horn must go.

Brutus' Last Song

Caesar's back, and they've built him a throne to sit on.
Get back to nature, Caesar. We've got you a tree stump;
broad as your kingly bottom. Magisterial.
Older than you'll ever be.
And when you rise from your wooden cradle,
black marks upon your robes'll tell
the people where you've been.

Ah, but when you sit now, that's really something.
See that bush, like a marvellous African head-dress
full of yellow whips, their tops dipped with blood;
or jugular red-hot pokers, who decided to take
a day off and wave a finger at your majesty.

Why, your majesty, see how, when you sit there,
they radiate around you.

One could almost believe you were going to die.

The Doll of Past Assurance

You are my bliss, do you know that?
The set of your bold deceit has washed out
my old unconcern. You've chipped

at my heart with such whimsy
and certitude it's performing
a gentle scream in the bowels

of my chest. The spies in your
fish tank have looked with dislike
on me, treading my way to your side

with love. The bronze of the framing
has flashed like a sword in
my mouth, deranging my speech.

By beds and cushions and candles, where
youthfulness sits and swells, I've lost
my style. I've lost my head, I've lost

my feet. I am holding the doll
of my old assurance and mirth
on the crown of my head. Many's

the bleached bone I am breaking now
in my unrelieved fury of soul.
Your house is my cradle of dreams

and ideas, my mothering kraal for
behaviour playful as rust. It allows me
my brushes and colours and leaves me

to think. The cross on the wall
is my second food. The spoonfuls
you offer increase me with heaven.

The platters of febrile meat have
excited my trust. Dear one,
am I dead now in terms

of your happiness? Has the wind rushed
through the feast depositing bones?
Have I broken the bread too hard

and too fast, finding a sexual tone
in an innocent lunch, scattering themes
of strong love by my covetous look?

Oh for the commune of pebbles we built
in the past. Oh for the buttered shared food
and the laughed-over poetry book.

Lovely Granaries

Come and visit my great big storage parlour.
It is ablaze with mice. The grain is sweetened
and bursting all over the floor till you'd risk
saying *flesh*. It disgorges light. My friend

the farmer thunders there, picking up sacks,
taking out his huge forefinger and making
indelicate love to the high drums. But he
never reaches the complete inside

of this beautiful granary before there comes
a knock at the door and he is off, off, being
a shark to the vermin. When he's gone –
first thing, there's a little shift. The small detail

of a miniature occupation begins to get known.
A shoot, a grimy move; the seed opens for a tail,
closes, smudges, girls with intractable eyes
would begin to bargain on a mouse. I've clipped

for you what they may look like. All this grey
doddering is beyond appreciation. It is *so*
unpleasant. Mouse to his friends goes kissing
anything that is excremental. Comradely Mr Fur

has his cheeks out with lemony grain
and excreta. The sole movement in
my beautiful granary is of pitching
skin cancer right through the neighbours.

Let me not infantly consider yellowy wheatgerm
to be the only story. The granary kips in my head
sometimes. It has florets of a skilled presentation
stocking the floor. And when my friend

the farmer comes, he is quite quite
heartened by the lucrative spilling body.
And when he stomps off hoeing, then
the mice begin to gnaw.

Books of Hours

There's a white-lipped lady
in a Netherlandish picture

I want to be. She has a book
which logically could not

possibly stay on her knee.
Visionary things are never

gravitational. Books with
Christ in go up and down

at an astonishing rate;
ladies sail without visible hair.

I'm a stick figure
in an age of bosoms

and frank atheism, would that
a book would flip from

my knee and start becoming
hungrily, angelically sweet.

Crabwise

This biting summer has brought out
pure chagrin in me. In your tumbled house
of icons and skulls, I have traced my demise

with a sure touch. The crab, bringing
a watering of salt to the freshwater fish,
has not more claws waved high in panic

than I, nor such a ticket of lust.
What have I done with you but gather bones
on a summer's night? The bleaching of teeth

discussed not only in our smiles.
I've stood with you over herbs and puddings,
questioning proportions and soil and feeling

the rough of your out-of-place silk
half an inch from my arm. Such
small things, breaking the air with no more

than indirection. I've a handful of shells
from the side of the lake that
we probably stood over like brothers,

getting wholly absorbed by the structures
they made. Dreadfully like brothers,
most woefully like friends of the same

merry sex, with the bird's head
of uncomplication twitching
its alternate eyes back and fro.

Is the silk of your tanned fingers
so purely for God on the tree? Is my carved
wearisome love for you so bald

as the dead gull's back? Is the bitten
quality of our eyes skirting
each other nothing more than a *lied*

no one will ever sing? A hornpipe that
calls in to dance just the bitumen gulls
on this beach's dry crust?

Der Hörende
(Toni Zenz 1957)

My metal arms touch at the elbows,
cramping the chest and pushing away
the emotions of the arteries.

My hands therefore splay out
like a pair of sugar tongs. Selecting
my cranium out of the servings

of bones and extending it upwards.
Curling my ears with their metal palms
and allowing the lobes to sink down

in a cushion around my backward
neck. These ears then have fought for
a new emphasis for themselves.

They have reared up out of
the sensory heap. They have
engineered for themselves

cavities, locking spiritual advice
under soft ledges, bringing
a feathery intonation

into the coils which work down
towards the drum. They have,
in the prettiest, most cursory way,

exhaled as receptors, presenting
themselves primarily to the odd voice
which sings from the brickwork in

moral notes. They have got a hold
on tenor passages of stunning good.
They have received word

of recondite annunciations,
peopling the middle air
with fiery future babes.

A Russian Farewell

Serge is saying goodbye
to his friend. There is

a black tenor of despair
about the instance. Music

may stop but the tenor
sings on, filling the atriums

of his absence with a round.
A round is like an inebriation

that has no end. Don't worry
friend. If the light goes,

we can rub our palms together
and press them to

the unmade hands on
the other side of the door.

Don't worry friend.
The men fall together

momentarily
like twinning bats.

Marian Hymn

Her goodness leaves scores on the skin
and all of that marital trousseau untouched.
Pictures in frames of herself that can
never come out, for she drags up the frames
to herself. No, she glances them there
with her toe. She hardly moves,
yet they come. Frames of the saint
and the virgin. Icons at least.
Devotional texts. Working the bloom
of the fame, of a babe without sex.
Curiously wan in the daylight.

Merely her hair is a signal to prayer,
or an invite for candles
to blacken and wreck. I want,
perforce, your mouth stopped from
this wonderland talk of umbrellas
and birds, this hiding in dells
of sly knowing silence;
this cotton! this wool! this
magnolia made to be kissed, bit
and left. I'll sue you at breakfast
for your freezing up eggs and then
chopping down men.

Girls Sitting Together Like Dolls

Judy likens the day with Elly,
to a cooking pot, to a steak full of juices, to
something their can lay their tongues on
and sweep along. And they
rustle their minds gleefully at this
secret metaphor.

Elly, making a pot of tea, calls it
a skull, that they may be drinking
from inside the pot. Judy loves
the idea of this good head syrup
they're getting down them.

The two girls create a crag of fruit
for every inch of their lovely skin.
Then they sit, realising everything is
not included. Elly slips
edibility into her perfect mind.

At the trial, when the judges asked where
was Elly, they found pips and stuff
in a trunk by the wall. They found Judy
at lunch on her quaint ways; on her
idiom of awkwardness, on her
artistic self.

The Ship of Faith

The lanterns on this heavenly ship
cake with something more than
literal light. Its oars address
the water like a finger down
from god inscribing form.
Irons jangle, bearing the weight
of angel feet, easy, white and
terrifying in their mass. The faces
of the good, mysterious women
look from the prow.

Faith holds the rudder on
this aggravating boat of dreams
I cannot board. Prudence loops
the strands of crystal hemp
around the helm. Good Fortitude
has shaved her head and stands
with fists, awaiting my arrival.
Bright Chastity has barred her doors
and rides the storm.

When this ship comes, as if often does,
from high medieval gloom toward
my beach, the scarlet of its wake
prevents my giving voice to
my support. Its sombre flag, depressed
then high, reveals the faitour in
my step of faith. Shadows
bringing the prow without
a sound to where I stand
denounce the cynic in
my rakish smile.

Anchors touch. These sterling girls
of Jesus have prevailed against the tide
as only angels can. Their laughter
is a thorn that brings me
swimming close. Enarmoured
like a knightish clown in platelets
wrought from sophistry and stain,
how damningly they add on weight,
the ladder finally dangling
near my sodden face.

And to this bird of speed
I never thought I'd come. Girls
grouping round in disbelief
to point the pallor in my eyes,
and brass corona of mendacity;
girls dressed like boys, demeanoured in
disdain, inclining forward to tamper
with the dead weight of my tread.

And on this ship it seems I cannot stay.
Girls make their homes here when they're good
and young, a chary queenhood
in their every move. My black soles
part the deck and pull my torso
down, throwing cross-sections
from this marine hulk of faith
up past my gaze. The layered loves,
the charming good, the rations
stacked in throes of meditation.
I stop at nothing. All this
skips me by. I stand on what
evaporates beneath my shoe.
My fingers rake the flying scenes
to find a hold. The ship's as nothing,
yes, as nothing. Why, its substance
gone to liquid. Rolled along
and scattered, quite craven in
its distance from my wanting hand.

Seahouses

The shells here are plain, toneless,
unextended by webs or
the horns of a sea-bottom court.
Rather they are stubs of things, holders
brutalised by being forgotten, scarred slices
of cell alleging to provide a rest for dull

amoebic guests. The beach has only
intermittently been kissed with
children's names. Birds condemned to gulp
extractions from the icy salt are more
the norm. Worms, leaving walkers cowed
by their sand tussocks, load

the damp corridor until the child's calls
and literatures find no room. The smell
of violent weed under sky spiked to
the full with grim intentions sends bathers
into an adamant retraction of their holiday bents
and vows. Sour, the islands not far out

hold only black birds now, but once
they harboured monks cut from their tribe,
wastrel goodmen at odds with the creed
of relation, sliding on dinghies of faith
to this offshore shelf. There, they saw
an accomplice for worship in gannets;

they hooked puffins in as readers
for their morning prayer. Perhaps
they eventually smouldered and finished
these birds as well, brought to a pass
by repetitive hunger. Perhaps they did not.
Moving their thin legs with difficulty,

perhaps they wove feathers to cover
a sandpiper's death. Cuthbert came here.
I know that he did. At war with the sight
of his followers, with the dimples and cushions
of Lindisfarne stone. He splayed out his hands
till they mastered the grip of the ruffian gull.

He collected the spray and wrote
manuscript notes on the calf of the rock.
They dried and went once he finished
a word. He reworked prayer into succinct
voiceless lots. It went flying up
in shells of purchase to the ocean god.

My Spirit, My Anger

My spirit, my anger, my unorthodoxy
all bound in one. It happens you have
given place to the severe girl with the cross
who holds a nunnery as her shooting-piece.

All love except love of God is grant
of the straw thing they keep to make
holes in. All elegance except curtains
and an unwilling slit for vision,

the badder way. I've seen beneath your hair,
to the unarticulated places of the skin,
which have sworn bone to the cause
of two, but hair and nimbus of hair

block every way out. There has been
licence, moments when we're saying nothing
and the cross becomes a tender sortie
into touching lines; moments

when the swan's feather becomes
a little sticky, a little numskull,
a little damp round the ears. Child,
it is as though someone had held

their huge hand over you, and you
had concentrated on singing hymns
about the stiffness of the fingers,
only to wake up and find

it was nothing but your own.
Erroneous Mary, the hair is
a pillow and not a war; one day
in your candour you will stay.

Primavera

Flora moved in, hanging
the Spring; it sat fleecing
and curled in the cribs

of her dress. The blue air:
everything gay, and that
basket of flowers

on her arm. Why
almost a flask; the flowers
melted and dolled themselves up

to be drunk. But I saw her face.
The eyes turned in, not out.
She hated this job of plant

resurrection. She knew
everything sad: how the roots
curled and ran from the soil

and the thin-veined plants sobbed
for their being there.
This pretty girl's cheeks

are rough with the madness
of serving again yellow fare,
of doling out old whiskied June.

Her mouth turns up in pain,
sketched by a sharp point.
She hates her own snare.

Morning Thesis

Sweetly breathed morning,
when you come over
the hill top as some steely

Lazarine monster, paring
oranges and oregano from
your fingernails, how often

you stop short on the summit
of the hill, hastily swallow
all the Pantheon smoke

you were preparing to exhale,
rearrange your metal facets
and cusps into reverse,

and scuttle away rearwards
executing a furtive sepulchral
courtship dance

back toward your
catacombs on the east
side of the world.

Sunflowers Tomorrow

Sunflowers have grown wings,
and are moving in harmony
with the spheres. So much so

their leaden heads and all
earthly vanity have been
put aside. They have ended

their courtship with oracular
globes of light and little girls;
yet remain, the bane of all,

cerebral and shortsighted,
gigantic penances in brown paper,
waving their tacit paternosters

at the dawn.

Rose Garden Ardour

1

There's someone too good in the garden.
I was down there the other night,
and it was no good, I fell,
near a haphazardly passionate plant.

He talked about worms, put
his strong fine hands over roses.
I spat like a flower under pressure
and flirted by touching the next bud.

When the grass grows long, will he
stop his soft absorption in the soil
and treat me like a cord he can
fragment and electrocute with

his sensitivity? Like a stem, ushered
into splinters lovingly? Like a brooch, pinned
on a leaf frighteningly, is my nimble
gaudiness matched with his silence.

2

I'm alight with a wicked way
of duality. There should only be
one set of paths lipped with
affectionate tardiness, grossness

and intense support. Now alongside,
like a joker stamping through the grass,
is the dextrous trail of choiceness
and seriousness, nibbling at me

with brilliant secrets. Supposing
my hands, hurdled between
his two at the rocked piano,
turned up and asked to close in with

the chords from his side, getting
landed on me runs and expressions
committed to magicking Pan just
a minute back; and a treatise with

this strange long silence of his began?
Where would be that ridiculous
hiccuping arbour, back on the road,
where I can buzz with poverty

and ugliness, and get pulled
by the wide arms of foolish goodness
into a cracked nest of maternity
somewhere below his chest?

Black Grain

You've gone, gone before going. How I hate
such an end, such a death. Like it nor not,
you have carried my skin with you

so my front is bloodied. You have
fed me with grain soaked in ink
so my mouth is black. You have scuttled

my hair and my skin and my eyes.
They grow shadows, they thin.
In the road of my thoughts, demolition.

Broken am I, of a damned heart. Pushed
to the floor in inelegant pain. Picked up
and pushed and assaulted and stripped,

and wet with the sweat of dissatisfaction.
Appealing, my mouth dried. Under paper moons
in the upstairs lounge my sentiment froze.

Sculptures have been cut out of ice of love.
This is the end of love. It has no veins;
its Bacchanalian start has been turned

towards wax. Your sombre mind, turning
excruciating wheels, metes out decline.
You write down the good

of disintegration. How can that be?
It reeks, it smells. Its behaviour,
which you say must be carried through,

leaves me dancing with wrath.
I anguish. Skilled in failure, I watch
your Olympian flesh turning away.

Homily

I am tissue paper thin,
shining like rain
and angry.
This is the third time
that God has not answered me.
I am fractious.

Behold me in the transept
early in the morning,
as white and ready to be
holy as bottled milk.

I am touchstone, I am
tinderbox. I will strike
my prayers off flint
to make them fly upwards –
I may have to push with
both hands.
I am holy milk, I am
trying to be good.

But you, robust pink stones –
just like the fathers,
with the dimples pressed into your cheeks
by an awareness of latent salt water.
You tell me nothing.
I have come here looking
for cordial,
and you tell me nothing.

There is nothing. Nothing but
the skeletal sunlight,
tapping its death certificate on
the priory gate.

The Grass Crust

You've pulled back, like
a shadow blackening over

the grass crust
and savaging the clarity

of things. Without a hint,
a long hold, or a kind

of savoury twilight where
the rip might leave

threads like hyphens
of old blood

on either side. Instead,
a snap at midday,

a little astronomical thing,
sloughing off the heart

and all contentment
with its asteroids of will.

On a Picture by Henry Moore

It seems now we're culled from tears.
The damp grained element has caught up
with us and given to our Arctic bone
and taut bodices something grimy

and abrasive. If I could, I'd concentrate
my gaze on your small round
upturned face gathered in a kind
of indignation and strength, but

the bruise marks beneath, marching
through your beautiful heart, insisting
on a connection with the other side
like a nip in a stem, maim me.

They set me back into an unhindered
curve, craning and peeping, but
gauchely, with the eyes put out. And on
my left side also, and around my blunt legs,

the chalk and the horrible painter's dust
have taken a hold. Where we fought
to retain some mutual, loving,
defensive whiteness, his face saw and hit

and worked into our organs. And I wince
as your collar bone creeps down, and my breast
is given savage lines. Keep your eyes
back from me. There is no possibility of us

falling together now. In that home,
in that cherished room where the sand
and light used to work together,
a new piece of legislation has appeared,

smarting and teasing the delicate borderland
between us. How can one resist
a statement from such a master.
Things which touched move slowly back.

Deer at Dawn

I can't remember much of it now.
Only the ragged vine branches –
mad and beautiful, like old women
abandoning their sterility.
The sunlight, still slippered,
shone inside each leaf,
illuminating and connecting
the glory to the glory.

The lawn was as sheer and blue
as ice. And hovering, with
the uncertain grace of a gull
three feet above the ground,
in the morning mist.
It cut one's throat, and only wanted
someone's blood to be perfect.

And then the deer got up.

The Trees of Vices and Virtues

These species start and finish in ink
on a sheep's hardened side. Leaves
fight for ground against the ghosts
of old wool. Some leaves curtsey

upwards, hard patches of faith
and prudence covering equal space.
Some wither in pain, pinned
by damning labels at their nodes.

Faceless trees; handless crucifixions;
sorties covering redemption
and aggression in a rush. They sway
through books, gathering up

the mind into a thing in soil;
and stamping out connections which
tend to polarise and sort and size
the scattered inclination. These trees,

ticked with unintelligible script,
are issues from the garden
of the page. Their context, furred
with sanctities, is sectioned

from psychology. The medieval writer,
rightly, took God and trees as
dual mentors, dual tools to chart
and sum the world. He weighed

the threatening forest down
with moral tags. He stopped
the anarchy of nameless leaves
before they'd yet unfurled.

Chicken by Water, New Mexico

Chicken had lost its seltzer and decided
to go for the next best substitute –
blessed Absalom – to knock-'bout-a-little
by the side of the water, dressed up
to look like old stone chicken feed.

Water paid its penny to come and see
chicken dance. Paternal water wanted
a son that looked just like chicken.
Says it was jus' ten clock in the morning
and sun was frying its bird feathers
on that handyman earth.

So chicken squeak and went for
cool, refreshing water. Tol' in the Bible
that Jesus came and needed a dip
before God gave him full God-like authority
to go, preach to unforgiven people.
Chicken is the daintiest of the birds,
so he put one foot in the water
and look down to see where he is going.

And no kidding, chicken saw this big,
this aggressive great bird. Could've come
out of anywhere. Noah's Ark, the zoo,
bird plantation – anywhere, he says.
Leaning forward to do the big guzzling
peck-peck that chicken doesn't like.

Shot off quick, chicken did; didn't want
nothing to do with the yellow big bird.
Says he thinks Jesus would have gone off
quick too, if he seen the big funny thing
that look nothing-at-all like him,
standing at the bottom of the lake.

The Climb Away from Flowers

The spring is now over. The way forward
lost its bright eyes a while back and groped
toward hardship, the landmarks of supernatural
repletion we'd hoped for ahead getting

sullied by strenuous art. I cradle no
handbook on how to proceed, when the lights
and eyes that were crayoned on the wall are
revealed to be fake. There is no guru climbing

out of a lotus flower, helped by a small cross,
in the sickly realism – unprotected by books –
I have opted to take. No hands are
holding me; the dropsy or any blasted germ

will not circle a radiance which I exude.
My state is exemplified by fishes which are
squeezed and die, lacking mythology. By love,
which bows and returns, noticing only what is

in front of its eyes. By a mad cloud, which
will not even stay an hour. When I walk out,
I am colliding with a June that has lost
faith in flowers and disbanded its succulent skies.

Skeleton Earth

He came, waving bones at me one night,
tapping out jigs on his palms; but they weren't
the bones of men – manageable things –
that live, die, and reappear, hunched
in the corners of doctors' waiting rooms,
vanishing at cockcrow. These bones have
finality; one can tell they're here to stay...

'Sir, there is a roundness and emptiness
about you that belies your stringy temperament.
Your openness astonishes me – things of this world
are generally obscure – but I can see
through you: transparent as the day.
Is that a star, sir, shining through the space
where your liver used to be? And upon your head –
I must admire it – a coronet of thorns? It is!
My, the poignancy of your sufferings fills me
with admiration; you must have been a martyr
or a saint, an emulation of our saviour.
With one difference: all your blood has drained away.
Excuse the question, sir, who drank it?'

'Bogmen from the East, my dear. They found
my soil absorbing. Not only that. My extra things –
all my little jewellery of rivers and forest sap,
were requisite. They picked cherries
from my mountains for their hats; drew
world maps with my fingers and shot Gurkhas
with my eyes. One or two things they were
wise enough to ignore – this delicate filigree
of tree roots you see, girdling my waist.

'Have you seen those Chinese ivory balls;
one inside the other, encompassing
a mysterious perfection. Ah well;
I was the error, the deviant, the one
they forgot to fill. No one had any stomach
for me after that. So they left me

rolling around on an ivory chessboard
without any pieces, under a dark blue sky
on the deep waters.

'One night at Christmas time, I will return;
oak trees and narcissi falling from me
like powder. When I laugh, men shall be
clothed in gold, and when I love wires
will break. I tell you the truth, they will
bleed tulips when I come...'

Dancing then, he missed his footing,
and shrieking down he fell.
This ball of roots and leaves and things,
lay broken as a bell.

Angels

What Thomist conceit saw them flaying
for balance on the head of a pin? That's
not right at all. The muscles in their
iridescent wings would be snagged
and their strong energies sapped by
such dry Latin games.

They're better in a garden. Gaining in
height and beauty even as we look.
Keeping pace with Rilke's comments
about radiance and terror, but full
also of a childlike reticence about
their errand, as they disappear behind
the topiary and re-emerge, their lips
obstinately tight,

passing the time of day anyhow.
Drumming their heels on
the tempera wattle as they loll back
and gaze abruptly into space, trying
to remember something, anything,
the suggestion of a quick task tossed
in passing over the shoulder
in that pre-picture whirl.

At last, lazily, while the girl – and we –
ache to know which flower it will be,
and which speck of soft visitation
within the womb, the miscreant
gives up his posture of absence
and attends to the task in hand. Hyacinth?
Auricula? No, it's the lily to beat all lilies
that he dabs gently from the soil
and turns on the diagonal, mounting
the steps before that outdoor, non-
perspectival prie-dieu with
growing certitude and charm.

The Pink Annunciation

Your lilies turn their opening mouths
my way. Whispering news devoid
of the chalk of virginity. Telling
a barbarous tale full of orange smoke.

They're purses of love, are they not?
Packed with a wandering dust hell-bent
to exhale. Many mornings, when
the straight little window I'm crammed under

hasn't even opened on my foul life,
they're right here – pervading the air with
forgetful honey, strutting their leafage
like a whore's routine, and holding

at bay that fine breath from the great
outdoors, where angels leave the line
dance they've been forming, and fight
to break through and get in.

Daybreak

From the top of this bank I am able
to examine the first line of the day.
Not even a paragraph, only a few
black squiggles and semi-colons
of faith that read out of the sky
to the dawn, abandoning grammar.

The word *blue* comes scuttling along,
executes a half bow and awkwardly
disappears. It is a very early word.
It dwelt here, crept around
and had independent yearnings
when the earth was still a fistful
of slivers and impulses. It
knows it and is ashamed.

Your tongue dampens your lips,
words are no longer necessary.
Overhead, the gloaming seems to
withdraw. All your loveliness
is clenched in strong white teeth
of foam, the grass becomes
wire at your signal
and the morning breaks.

Milking

Caught like animals, young goats
on God's left hand, we lay our heads
together, exploring the ladder
of smells from groin to throat.

So many places to sit and nuzzle
the garlands of wrenching primrose,
so many places to slide one's
serious nose up a flowery creek.

I have pitched my tent on
the lowest rung, where the milk
has the sweetest stench
and most generously runs, making

pails bonny with its moisture,
taking the monopoly from
all those summer's day heifers
apparelled in marital brown.

Sheep are the ones that God loves;
not cows, not goats. Up to
the knees in goodness and milkless
chatter. Yet their wool doesn't

grab me at all, No, that tangle
of energy, mixing canvas, ladders
and horned heads is where I'm
pinioned in guilt, and where

I squat in my cloven vestments
sampling unlegislated milk.

Renaissance

1

It is when lily shoots break
a path through concrete,
and when a dead tree stump
has small green people invading it.

It is after a storm when white leaves
have been plastered into the soil.
And something elastic returns.

Most of all it has to do with   •
an unhindered dove
and a splash of water.

2

When the sun looks
the mountains are like blisters
and the sea is a tiny curl of the tongue.

When the moon looks
he sees white eyes with black pupils
staring at him through the dark.

When Jesus looks
he sees only one hill
and a sponge soaked in wine.

3

So seeds are sown
and the old gardener straightens his back.

He has spent an age considering
the plot, exploring the lie
of the land, pulling up trees

with either hand, sitting on his haunches,
and becoming a part of
the landscape to small wild creatures.

At last he crouched over a point
where the soil was as light
and as frail as mist, and where
a lily grew protectingly. By its roots
he ground his thumb round
through the dust to make a hollow,
and blew the membrane from his forehead
into the hole. By his beard
he covered it up, and with his tears
he watered it.

4

Caves have a reputation for harbouring strange things,
and this one was no exception as the woman found
when she approached.

Although she had risen early, the dawn light
was just beginning to appear round the hill.

By it, she saw the water,
and it was making love to the stones,
allowing them to shift slightly in the stream.

By it, she saw that there were
no birds in the trees.

By it, she saw small stones and animals,
stilled like children in prayer.

And by it, she saw the cave had said goodbye
to the boulder placed in front of it, and that
the boulder was standing a little way off
looking for all the world as if it knew exactly
what kind of controversy it was going
to cause in the history books.

5

We had all given the clock up for lost.
Father was a clockmaker
but he shook his head sadly
and mother summoned us children to bed.
'There's nothing more you can do,' she said,
and hustled father up too.

Out of the bedroom window,
the evening sky still had scratches
of old sunlight left on it, and the city
glittered like tempered brass.
Before we slid between the sheets,
the curtains still seemed to maintain
a slight glow.

Deep into the night
a peculiar clear chime
like a church bell
pierced us
from the room downstairs.

Counting Bones

Love skips to attention, putting down
her banknotes of prudence and sanctuary light.
She stands by the door or is watching
the phone, blue at the eye, counting
the bones in her wrist and the days
till the night.

Loves stands at the door, with skirts of
the Holy Bible at half mast round her knees.
With taboos in a bin in the back room
and the wreck of the ship of good purpose
overturned in dark seas.

Loves stands at the door, awaiting the one
that she loves. She is living on nothing
but fire and air. Her books are all lost,
her precepts and mottos gone green with
disproving and God is not there.

Is God not there? Under a new sky
a doorbell rings. He has come. He has come.
His hands hold a pageant of sexual wealth;
in his mouth lies repletion with gilded teeth.
His neck is encircled with felony's drum.

This is love. This is he. All else is a blank.
In the fields of their bed give respect to
their tree. Its roots are in nothing. Its branches
lift high. It has grown without light yet it
sunders the sky.

Losing Heart

I may have lost heart, and knowing this,
bought myself a crate with an amazing
inclusiveness as far as love is concerned.
I may have opened a panel and, seeing
this old romantic thing with little scrawls
of pure trust and exaltation had mildewed,
have gone for an optionless style someone once
held up to me in the pragmatic schools.

A board full of lightless apertures,
dubbed with a bleak, dutiful welcome;
a trench with something unrelishable
at the bottom, which I was moved
to create out of stiff compromise.

Convent Thoughts 1992

Nothing, in this big house, has a line
put through it in a straight way. Instead,
there's an option for lard in white chunks
as a layer over fuss. Nothing I've heard
comes with pincers,

like a lean prayer moving up a glass wall
purposefully. More, the stertor of
nuns giving orders so deceitfully
flares into lyrics, that everything's lulled
and the progress of two points stops.

The church upstairs is emptier than this
greased stitching with tracts. Sometimes
it drops pictures off the walls when
it doesn't like their worldview. It has mats
and slabs which repeat the monosyllables

of words of prayer. They shouldn't really be
exposed alone, they are only the start of
a column that ends in a luminous ventricle.
And it has crucifixes, executing
right angles, which underwrite the air.

Between the geometry and the lithe flecked
sprawling cream carried by nuns
in large jugs, is an area in parentheses
where I keep pulling on my ugly clothes
and don't change. Here I urge murder,

and circle the kitchen, curdling soup and
touching up milk suspiciously. I make love
with glances at hardly animate things and size up
nuns behind their backs as though conducting
sketches for a seamless execution garment.

Facing

Sweetness left me on the line
a while back. Hips, jowls,
the murderous onset of fat
charged in and scoured
my skinny frame. Where is

the girl with the silken left shoulder
and melamine skin? Where is
that dainty whose purpling stare
extracted male sin?
If, in the mirror, I see

an unlikeable face, how soon
before should this interest have
stopped and turned tail
to my soul instead, augmenting
the good and the heartfelt wish,

the spidery grin of sheer love;
and shrugging aside the drag
of the mouth, and the anxious, fly-blown eyes
of this silvered doll? When heaven arrives
with its sack full of years

and probably drooling too,
this uncertain front – which is
all I am – will recoil from
the courage required of the old.
The hole in the face the teeth

have left, offering wordless religion;
the slip of the eyes to the right
and left, tendering sacrosanct smiles
through their singlet of cold.
Where is the wash that will

start me anew, and finish
that dastardly mirror of sight?
Bring me the dove with
the sop in its bill and sparkling
basket of grooming tools.

I'll tread in his garner of hyssop
without a qualm. I'll rake
the cheeks of my excess
with scions of praise. The herbs
of the season shall press

to my ardourless nose. Throw out
from the heavens all the thrushes
and finches and bring me
in a birdcage of silver
that snowy young cove.

Hourglasses

Hourglasses read as the feminine body on show;
each piece of sand as nard, tears, wiry resolution,
or the iron in the small of the back. But the belt

where time is lovingly confined by the minute
I want to undo, to shimmy down the escalator
of old years, find eighty-three and strong earth eager

to give me a break. Blow this holding back
of the insidious grain. Who can get inside
the hourglass and make it a tube? I'm calling on him

to visit me, to cosset the glass away from
its curves. I'm calling on a spoon-bender
to exchange his profession for the night.

I'm calling on dwarves with torches and staffs
to build me into their fire. When everything's
molten we're in for a gush. Oh, beautiful flakes.

Here's where my granny begins, in the flakes
of her old face; here's gurgling and bile
in bad city gardens. Here's a powder that is

deftly ripped from that old man's paunch.
Here's the aspect of dustbins I don't like.
Here's my beautiful arm, quite gone in a coil,

with the hand raving back to the shoulder.
So, sweet, come with your gifts and your stout pocket-knife
and let's quicken this gathered-in waist of a life.

Grip

Your grip is still upon me, over the sea,
touching my ear with brotherliness
and refusing awe, strong with a plain

pleasure that reaches as far as it should
and then stops. I wish that someone
with a frown would slacken your strings

and send you roaring to me.
I remember an older year, shot through
with belief, when restraint was an old hen

we sent laughing from the door.
I remember being unscared by the stealthy gait
of withdrawal she displayed. I remember

the bold way I slated amor, thinking
she would fix her lovely hands on me
till the dues of a lifetime were paid.

Playing the Violin

There's a crawling animal in the bottom
somewhere. It scuddles at Mozart
and snores at Beethoven. Its eyes
are as black and sticky as caviare,
and in between is its snout.

'Mercy, little bear, little fable, or whatever
I am fated to call you.
Stay if you must, but come out if you can.
I shall then play such music
that you will be glad you went away.'

It still remains; gently nuzzling the wood,
occasionally chopping. And its eyes
never grow dim as it follows the fall
of my bow, and as it preens itself,
mocking.

Violin by Night

What violin, stretching itself beneath your confident hands,
can draw such hearty breath? What veneer,
quickened to gold by the daily sleep with your
collar-bone, has shone with as much pleasure?
The bow drawn over me has been tightened
with stealthy bolts which make me sing.
The bronze of the largo you wring out in gasps
gives the tempo for which I have always longed.

From where, silver with effort, did we find
such felicitous score? Was it set down today,
or is it some love-child of Ovid's, exhumed from
a classical night? It plays in our dual breath –
your breath a lance on the wood, my breath
pouring with blood – like choice love –
rapt fruit, sin and pearls. Like censored
libretto exposed to the light.

No one I've known can play the dear fiddle
so neatly as you. The look as you do is
the thing I have always wanted to see and
I see it now; smiling away at the wood as you
bring it to life; turning and tuning and
shifting the strings of my sycamore heart.
Here it is then. The fiddle beneath,
the great brooding haunch of the man up above,
coursing his way down the spine of
the catgut of love.

Noah's Ark Demoralised

The madness of the church! An enclave
of scholars and camels huddled together,
with the water picking its way through all
the delights of the world outside, and the rain
lashing upon those hapless planks
of congregation with what only a divine
persistence of purpose can really achieve.

The sweet little animals, holding up
under the weather, but riled internally
at their segregation into appetite
and rationality, and prone to bouts
of lassitude. The birds, however,
secretly delighted to be gelled with
the things of the spirit, bowling up
into the rafters and vying for
olive-branch status, not to speak
of a stretch in the Trinity.

That Noah then! Who can he be?
Racked with an amateur sailor's
cough and fluttering with cold.
He's a pattern for god on
a human scale. Encumbered
with nightmares of mishap he
keeps us on course. The swell
of the waves makes the shape
of the cross to his agonised mind.
The blond doves of meekness
he waves on their way wear
a neckring of moralised force.

A new heaven and a new earth...
there was no longer any sea

Mornings make me feel Venusy, I rush down
to the sand and send a sacrifice of laughter
to my mother's legs. The breaking thighs,
the trough with the cockle, the lather of flowers

using the air like soil. While it's still light
I complete my pagan business, pull out
any man that I love and crunch his dryness
on the grazing sea. Bracket his feet

with my fierce legs, lock his knees
in a water belt, and pelt him with fish tales
till suddenly I've made a haul to the sea-bed
and am treasuring his thick glasses

and salt rash under a stone. Mornings speckle him
under the sea with a lack of gods, except
my enormous heart, moueing and thudding
to gain his devoted stare. Fish which used

to be content with holidaying in gold coats
have now spun out line in their own right
and fit us together, eye to eye, until everything
even the garrisoned germ of sight spills out

on that liquid connecting nylon. Carp are
the hope of the world at this needlework.
They have mothers who kicked out of nets
alive and taught them the ropes. They have

martyrs who haplessly sent their bones up
to the needle trade, making free spirits insane
with the rickety score of their stitches.
My eyes are lit with opacity. I light on

myself in a flash of unflattering truth.
The sexual thing is so brief; it's like
making kids from my hand's clash with
my eye. No. The wrecking, alluring thing

you have is my garnet self, formed from
your nerves and faith and embarrassed love.
It's bullion for one; it's the cinder
I've scratched for which stays priced.

Give it me, lest you suddenly
see it as sand, and your heart
goes brown. God is the mote
in this agreeable seeing and pulling

at sea. He bawls in, making the fish
look like crosses, making the carp
all aglow with radiant love, making
your eyes cease filling with water

and reflecting me hopelessly. He calmly
shafts Venus and blows her onshore,
rendering void her voluptuous slide.
Venus is not just that ridiculous vice

of overgrown breast which we've spotted
and chucked. She's more the surmise
of completion engendered by me facing you,
which chirrups that heaven is four legs.

She's a remnant of humanism, who pulled in
amazing returns from her tracts; a Lorelei maiden
poised, arms akimbo, mouth open to
sing out a throatful of waterside facts.

*

I'm there in the morning again, a more
reticent day, the sky overzealous and damp
with good works. My Venus has sheared off
her hair and reordered her legs, releasing

the catch of the past and her ardent
unchristian grasp. She expires on the sand
like a beached thing, rebuffing the waves
and staring inland. Her men are elsewhere

and are old now, repenting their nautical days
in some clerical pile. The flowers of the air
have no more amoral glee to buoy up
their height. Released from their

pink and white moorings they sink
to the sea, observing the colour reduce
from their wings, like the onset of ominous
brown in an insect's last flight.